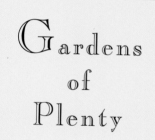

Gardens
of
Plenty

GAIL GRECO'S
LITTLE
Bed & Breakfast
COOKBOOK SERIES

Gardens of Plenty

Text by GAIL GRECO

Photographs by TOM BAGLEY

RUTLEDGE HILL PRESS
Nashville, Tennessee

Published in Nashville, Tennessee, by Rutledge Hill Press, Inc., 211 Seventh Avenue North, Nashville, Tennessee 37219. Distributed in Canada by H. B. Fenn & Company, Ltd., 34 Nixon Road, Bolton, Ontario L7E 1W2. Distributed in Australia by Millennium Books, 33 Maddox Street, Alexandria NSW 2015. Distributed in New Zealand by Tandem Press, 2 Rugby Road, Birkenhead, Auckland 10. Distributed in the United Kingdom by Verulam Publishing, Ltd., 152a Park Street Lane, Park Street, St. Albans, Hertfordshire AL2 2AU.

Editorial assistance by Tricia Conaty
Photo prop assistance by Camden Pottery of Camden, Maine, and Butler's Orchard of Damascus, Maryland
Photo film processing by Berry and Homer of Lanham, Maryland
Cover and book design by Gore Studio, Inc.
Text layout and typesetting by John Wilson Design

ON THE FRONT COVER: GARDENS OF PLENTY AT SETTLERS INN. RECIPES FROM LEFT: ONION YOGURT TART WITH CALENDULA PETAL, FOUR-GRAIN VEGETABLE AND NUT SALAD WITH MAPLE VINAIGRETTE; COUSCOUS VEGETABLE SALAD WITH CHILI LEMON DRESSING

Library of Congress Cataloging-in-Publication Data

Greco, Gail.
    Gardens of plenty / text by Gail Greco : photographs by Tom Bagley.
       p.   cm.
    Includes index.
    ISBN 1-55853-474-1 (hardcover)
    1. Cookery, American. 2. Bed and Breakfast accommodations—United States. I. Title.
TX715.G811468 1997
641.5—dc21
                                      97-4470
                                         CIP

Printed in the United States of America

1 2 3 4 5 6 7 8 9 — 00 99 98 97

Other Books in This Series

Vive la French Toast!
Autumn at the Farmers Market
Chocolates on the Pillow
Recipes for Romance
Tea-Time Journeys

Contents

About the Recipe Test Kitchen viii

MORNING GLORIES
1

SHADOWS ON
THE SUNDIAL
23

FIREFLIES AN D
CANDLELIGHT
39

Stuffed Bell Peppers with Vegetables and Tofu

Salmon with Dill Lemon Sauce

Chicken Flowerpot Pies

Rhubarb and Walnut Bread

Chocolate Garden Beet Cake with Vanilla Sauce

FOR THE LOVE OF VEGETABLES
57

Spaghetti Garden Ragout

Fiddleheads and Fettuccine

Vegetable Stroganoff

Roasted Vegetable Galette

Tuscan Bean and Vegetable Soup

Vidalia and Rhubarb Ratatouille

Savory Tomato Cobbler

MUCH A-DEW ABOUT HERBS
73

Basil Soup

Fresh Mint and Pea Soup

Smoked Chicken and Sage Pinwheels

Herb-Crusted Pork with Apricot Sauce

Bow Ties Vegetarian with Walnut Pesto

Lemon Thyme Potato Pancakes

Herb-Scented Stuffed Onion Saucers

Rosemary Biscotti

POSIES FOR THE PALATE
91

Lemon Flower Pancakes with Pansy Butter

Potato and Herb Soup with Calendula

Chilled Spiced Peach Soup with Floating Violets

Orange and Poppy-Seed Biscotti

Buttermilk Lavender Bread

Onion Yogurt Tart with Calendula Petals

Flower Petal Pound Cake

Lavender Cookies

The Test Kitchen for the Cooking Association of American Inns

Although all inn recipes are tried-and-true and served at the inns all the time, the recipes in this cookbook have been further verified and tested for accuracy and clarification for the home kitchen.
The cooking seal of approval that accompanies this book, means that every recipe has been tested in inn kitchens other than the source, and that the association test kitchen has been satisfied that the recipe is proven and worthy of preparing.
The test kitchen is under the leadership of association founder Gail Greco.
The prestigious list of kitchen testers includes:

CAROL COVITZ EDMONDSON, *Chef/Owner*
The Captain Freeman Inn • Cape Cod, Massachusetts

DENNIS HAYDEN, *Chef/Owner*
Blue Harbor House • Camden, Maine

JUNE KLEMM, *Chef/Owner*
Boxwood Inn • Lancaster, Pennsylvania

PATRICK RUNKEL, *Chef/Owner*
October Country Inn • Bridgewater Corners, Vermont

TODD SEIDL, *Chef/Owner*
Victorian Treasure • Lodi, Wisconsin

CHRIS SPRAGUE, *Chef/Owner*
The Inn at Ormsby Hill • Manchester, Vermont

LAUREL TESSIER, *Chef*
The Notchland Inn • Hart's Location New Hampshire

Gifts from the Good Earth

Gardens seem to have all the answers. Even the solutions to some of our personal dilemmas may be found after a stroll through a garden. Life began in a garden, it is written. And so, life continues in a garden, not only figuratively but literally. Some of our most treasured recipes are created from the virtuous plantings proudly sprouting their tasty offerings: corn so sweet you could nibble it off the cob and backyard tomatoes so ripe and juicy they don't even need the olive oil and basil.

Gardens are giving. With the turn of the soil and a period of nurturing, they bring forth gifts for the kitchen. In that vein, planting and growing something in the dirt brings rewards for the labor extended. A garden teaches us about love.

While we look to the garden to plan what to put on the stove, we also find much more during our fruitful rummaging. And that is what *Gardens of Plenty* is all about—a recipe book that has been carefully planted with the seeds of a

nourishing table at home. It will also serve to fertilize those seeds with the essence of the garden: creativity, simplicity, and celebration.

Great recipes are plowed with ingredients that are fresh, methods that are easy, and combinations that are festive—beginning with the break of day, when the morning glories are at their daily peak, ushering in a flood of hope and revival. So the "Morning Glories" chapter has cooking ideas that beckon you to look at things in a new light: perhaps a French toast made with tomatoes and ham, or muffins sprouting from flowerpots that seem to cradle the bread. By the way, bed-and-breakfast inns are always caressing the soul and yet at the same time pushing the mind and heart to grow beyond the usual sphere—gardens and inns, growing and nurturing—they are symbiotic.

There are very few inns I know that do not have an herb patch. Even we home cooks have at least an herb or two growing on the porch or on the windowsill. So, when the dew glistens, the world awakens, and rosemary perfumes the air, it may be a day to make a savory herbal biscotti or perhaps a little meal of dough filled with sage and chicken swirled up like a pinwheel from the "Much A-Dew about Herbs" chapter.

As the day continues to brighten, even the flowers begin to arouse notions of what might indulge the day's table—from flower-petal pancakes to hearty soups and sweet cookies. Historically, "Posies for the Palate" have always sparked the cook's imagination, and they do so even now as you will discover in the chapter by that name. Flowers are experiencing a renaissance of recipes celebrating their tastes and vibrant colors.

As afternoon shines down on the garden, it is time for simple tastes like those in the "Shadows on the Sundial." Here you will find such midday ideas as buckwheat-and-fennel bread with a lemon squash soup. After lunch, the garden exhilarates with a ripening of vegetables. Some of those picked will be used fresh, while others will be put up for the giving all winter long with recipes from "For the Love of Vegetables."

When the sun sets, the fireflies are not enough to light the meal at the table. But pair them with candlelight and you can show off the day's choice of crisp toast rounds with cheese and sautéed vegetables, flowerpot pies, and garden beet cake from the "Fireflies and Candlelight" collection of recipes.

A conspiracy of ingredients makes up recipes that respond to all these daily changes in the garden, and they are all here in this book. Secrets from the cooks of bed-and-breakfast and country inns combine with suggested dishes from my own recipe box, offering many reasons to celebrate our gifts of the good earth.

If you do not have a garden, you can visit one at an inn. Putting this book together gave me the chance to explore the details of many an inn's garden. These are gardens where you are invited to live during your stay, and not just as a tourist on the sidelines, unable to touch, feel, and smell. And at an inn, you can truly taste what grows in the garden. At one inn I visited, guests go out every day with the chef and help pick the produce that will be on the table only minutes later.

Gardens of plenty abound at inns, where the cycle is complete. Flowers and produce grow in abundance. Meals are inspired by the good, giving earth and are then placed before the guest with beauty, grace, and invitation.

But when you cannot be in one of these gardens, it is okay to fantasize. So, I will leave you with a passage from *Brother Juniper's Bread Book.* Author Peter Reinhart shows us his fantasy about breadmaking. It could apply to nearly any dream we have about producing food for the table, including spending time in a garden:

"I gather the wheat, corn, rice, and oats from local fields, grind them myself in a stone mill, make a dough by adding milk just taken from the resident cow or ewe, and sweeten it with honey extracted from one of the many beehives that we keep to pollinate the fields. Then I bake the bread in a brick oven fired by local hardwood and bring the still-hot loaf to the local holy elder for a blessing. After that I share the loaf with friends, strangers, and the poor. This is bread, the consolidation of all that is harvestable and all that is good about life on this earth."

Morning Glories

Next time you make baked apples, take your basic recipe and add raisins and a teaspoon of minced fresh mint to each apple. Great for breakfast!

Sweet Melon Soup with Citrus and Wine

Light and sophisticated, this soup is beautiful in clear bowls or crystal stem glasses. The soup may be prepared the night before and in fact needs a chilling time of at least three hours. Our testers tried this without the corn syrup and with very ripe melon, and found the taste just as sweet. Season with a bit more salt, however.

3	large cantaloupe, peeled, seeded, and cut into chunks		2	large honeydew melons, peeled, seeded, and cut into chunks
³/₄	cup freshly squeezed orange juice		½	cup fresh lime juice
1	cup dry white wine			Fresh mint leaves for garnish
⅓	cup light corn syrup			

MAKES 8 TO 10 SERVINGS

In a food processor, combine the cantaloupe, orange juice, ½ cup of the wine and 4 tablespoons of the corn syrup. Purée until smooth. Strain and transfer the mixture to a

pitcher. Clean the processor bowl and add the honeydew, the remaining wine, remaining corn syrup, and the lime juice. Purée until smooth. Strain and pour the mixture into another pitcher. Chill both purées for at least 3 hours. Stir the contents of each pitcher before serving. Pour both melon mixtures into a large glass bowl simultaneously. Garnish with fresh mint leaves.

—THE INN AT CEDAR FALLS

PICTURE FACING CHAPTER OPENER: BREAK OF DAY SHINES BRIGHTLY ON THE BREAKFAST TABLE AT NOTCHLAND INN.
LEFT: A MOMENT IN TIME FOR AN EARLY-DAY BLOSSOM: THE MORNING GLORY

Blueberry Biscuits

∽o∾

Light and airy, these savory biscuits are delicious with lemon curd at the breakfast table. Blueberries are too difficult to cultivate in the average garden at home, but if you are lucky enough to have them growing in a nearby orchard, run out and pick every last one (with the owner's permission, of course).

2	cups sifted all-purpose flour		2	tablespoons shortening
1	tablespoon sugar		³/₄	cup milk
4	teaspoons baking powder		2	tablespoons light molasses
¹/₂	teaspoon salt		³/₄	cup fresh blueberries

MAKES 10 TO 12 BISCUITS

Preheat the oven to 350°. Sift the flour, sugar, baking powder, and salt into a large mixing bowl. Cut in the shortening. Add the milk and molasses gradually, mixing well until a dough begins to form. Stir in the blueberries. Transfer the dough to a

lightly floured surface, and roll out to about 1 inch thick. Press out the biscuits with a 2¹/₂-inch biscuit cutter, making sure to use all the dough. Arrange the biscuits on a lightly greased baking sheet. Bake for 20 to 25 minutes, or until golden brown.

—GAIL'S KITCHEN

ABOVE: WHICH WAY WILL THE DAY GO? AN ANTIQUE WHIRLIGIG AT OCTOBER COUNTRY INN KNOWS THE ANSWER.

Tomato and Cheddar Baked French Toast

﹏

Our testers also made this recipe with eggplant and red peppers instead of bacon and provolone instead of cheddar.

At Cambridge House B&B, innkeeper Tony Femmino makes a great breakfast—Italian style. The asparagus marinara egg dish, on page 12, is served with his Italian sausage that has a garden accent: Mix together 3 pounds (95 percent fat free) boneless pork loin coarsely ground with 3 tablespoons Kosher salt, 2 teaspoons cracked pepper, and 2 tablespoons fennel seeds. Form 2-inch patties (³/₄-inch thick) and sauté in extra virgin olive oil over medium heat until golden. Top each patty with 3 to 4 drops freshly squeezed lemon juice for added flavor.

8	1-inch slices whole-wheat French bread	1	12-ounce can evaporated skim milk
1	tablespoon or more butter melted	1/4	teaspoon freshly cracked black pepper
8	slices Canadian bacon	5	Roma tomatoes, sliced (about 1 pound)
3/4	cup grated sharp Cheddar cheese		Petite yellow or orange marigold petals for garnish
4	eggs, beaten		

MAKES 4 SERVINGS

*P*reheat the oven to 350°. Coat a 13x9-inch glass baking dish with cooking oil spray. Arrange the French bread in the dish and brush with melted butter as desired.

Place the bacon over the bread and top with 1/2 cup of the cheese.

In a mixing bowl, combine the eggs, milk, and black pepper. Mix well. Slowly pour the mixture over the bacon.

Bake uncovered for about 15 minutes or until firm. Remove the pan from the oven and arrange the tomato slices over the top. Continue baking for an additional 10 minutes. Sprinkle the French toast with the remaining cheese while still warm. Serve as is—warm and melting—and garnish with marigolds, if desired.

—DIAMOND DISTRICT B&B

LEFT: MINIATURE MARIGOLDS, EDIBLE INGREDIENTS FOR A NUMBER OF GARDEN-STYLE RECIPES, INCLUDING THIS ONE

Strawberry Cantaloupe Omelet

୨୦~

The pairing of the eggs with fruit (instead of vegetables as in a Western omelet) makes this dish a fresh-from-the garden medley. The sweet berries, with the melon and the eggs, cleanse the palate. Delicious accompanied by the blueberry biscuits on page 5.

1/4	teaspoon olive oil
3	eggs
1	ounce water
1/4	teaspoon baking powder
3	medium strawberries, hulled and thinly sliced
1/4	ripe cantaloupe, peeled, seeded, and sliced equally into 6 3/4-inch pieces
1/4	teaspoon powdered sugar

MAKES 1 SERVING

*H*eat the olive oil in a nonstick skillet. In a small bowl, combine the eggs, water, and baking powder. Beat well. Pour the egg mixture into the hot skillet. Using a rubber spatula, move the eggs around in the pan to ensure even cooking. When the

mixture is set, flip the omelet to brown on its reverse side.

Arrange 1/2 the strawberry slices and 1/2 the cantaloupe slices on the top side of the omelet. Fold the eggs over the fruit. Slide the fruit-filled omelet onto a serving plate. Garnish with remaining fruit and powdered sugar.

—THE LITTLEPAGE INN

Stuffed Pears with Rosemary Honey

∽∘∾

Innkeeper and cooking class instructor Joan Morris was inspired by cookbook author Marion Cunningham in developing this recipe. What a cheerful way to start the day. You need to prepare the honey at least one week ahead of time. Reserve the remaining honey for future recipes.

I love dried hydrangeas. When the blossoms are ready to harvest, place them in a car trunk and close the lid. Park the car in a spot that will get sun all day. After 24 hours, check to see whether they are dried; if not, leave in the trunk again, until completely dried.

Rosemary Honey				
1	pint jar light honey		1/2	cup lightly toasted walnuts, coarsely chopped
2	sprigs fresh rosemary		3	tablespoons sugar
Pears			1	tablespoon fresh lemon juice
8	small Seckel pears (or Bosc), peeled		**Sauce**	
1/3	cup golden raisins		1/4	cup rosemary honey
			1/4	cup water

MAKES 8 SERVINGS

*P*repare the rosemary honey. Remove the lid from the honey jar and place jar in the microwave. Heat on high for 1 minute. Place the rosemary sprigs into the jar of warm honey. Cover and allow the flavors to meld for 1 week. Check the flavor of the honey, adding more rosemary if needed. (Allow 1 week for each addition of rosemary.

Store extra honey for another recipe.) When honey is ready, use a melon baller, and carefully core the pears from the bottom, leaving the outer stems intact. Set aside. Preheat the oven to 350°. In a small bowl, combine the raisins, walnuts, sugar, and lemon juice. Fill the cavity of each pear with the raisin-walnut mixture.

Arrange the pears upright in an 8x8-inch glass or ceramic baking dish, making sure that the pears fit snugly. Combine the rosemary honey with the water; pour over the pears. Bake for about 45 minutes or until the pears are soft. Serve warm or at room temperature with extra rosemary honey.

—THE NUTHATCH B&B

ABOVE: A STILL LIFE FROM THE BARN AT OCTOBER COUNTRY INN HINTS AT THE DAY AHEAD.

Petite Asparagus Frittatas
with Marinara Sauce

❦

Italian-style breakfast is served at the inn on various Sunday mornings when guests have time to linger over good food. This dish was a total surprise, and served with the zeppole (pictured at far right; recipe on page 17), it makes a delicious Sunday evening snack as well. Substitute with a 28-ounce can of quality crushed tomatoes if Romas are not in season.

Serve this cilantro pumpkin-seed butter from the Nuthatch B&B on plain cornmeal muffins: To 1 ½ sticks unsalted butter, mix in 1 ½ large garlic cloves, minced, ½ cup toasted and minced salted pumpkin seeds, and ⅓ cup (packed) minced cilantro leaves.

Sauce		Asparagus	
4	tablespoons extra virgin olive oil	1	pound asparagus, woody ends snapped off
2	cloves fresh minced garlic	**Frittata**	
2	pounds fresh Roma tomatoes, skinned, seeded, and finely chopped	8	extra-large eggs
		1	roasted red sweet pepper, cut into 1/2-inch chunks
1	tablespoon oregano	2	tablespoons grated Parmigiano-Reggiano cheese
1/2	teaspoon salt		
1/2	teaspoon freshly cracked pepper		Salt and freshly cracked pepper
2	tablespoons fresh-chopped basil leaves	1/4 to 1/2	cup extra virgin olive oil

MAKES 4 TO 6 SERVINGS

*H*eat 2 tablespoons of the olive oil in a large heavy skillet and sauté the garlic for 1 to 2 minutes. Add the tomatoes, oregano, salt, and pepper. Simmer 10 minutes, stirring occasionally. Remove from the heat and stir in the basil. Just before serving, add the remaining 2 tablespoons of the oil.

While the sauce cooks, prepare the asparagus. Peel outer skins of asparagus. Cut each stalk into 1-inch lengths. Lightly steam the asparagus cuts; run under cold water and drain; set aside.

Assemble the frittata. Beat the eggs in a large bowl. Add the asparagus, red pepper, and cheese. Season with salt and pepper. Coat the bottom of a heavy skillet with oil and heat over medium high about 1 to 2 minutes. When the oil is heated through, pour 2 generous serving-size spoonfuls of batter to form 2 (3-inch) frittatas. After 15 seconds, turn the frittatas over to cook on the other side. The frittatas should be cooked to a light golden brown. Continue making frittatas until all of the batter is used up. Remove from the pan and place layered on a serving plate. Serve with the sauce and zeppole.

—A CAMBRIDGE HOUSE

*F*eta *Veggie Pie with*
Rolled Oat and Wheat Germ Crust

∽∾

Don't be intimidated making this crust. It will look great no matter how you roll it. The crust truly adds to the texture of this pie that overtly tastes of herbs and Feta cheese in the midst of the eggs.

Make a viola salad the way they do at Wildflower Inn. Mix together 4 Roma tomatoes, a large Vidalia onion (sliced), a cup of black olives, 8 ounces string cheese pulled apart, and a tablespoon of chopped chives. Add a vinaigrette dressing and top with lots of violas or Johnny-jump-ups.

Crust

2	cups whole-grain bread crumbs
1	cup organic wheat germ
1	cup rolled old-fashioned oats
$1/2$	cup whole-wheat flour
$1/2$	teaspoon marjoram or basil
1	cup extra virgin olive oil

Filling

12	eggs
1	cup plain yogurt (or sour cream)
1	cup milk
1 to 2	teaspoons minced fresh basil, marjoram, tarragon, or dill
1	teaspoon garlic salt
	Freshly cracked black pepper
3	cups vegetable combination of carrots, green peppers, onions, and zucchini, cut julienne
	Olive oil for sautéing
1	cup crumbled Feta cheese
	Paprika

MAKES 8 TO 10 SERVINGS

*P*reheat the oven to 400°. Prepare the crust. In a large bowl, combine the bread crumbs, wheat germ, oats, whole-wheat flour, and marjoram. Add the olive oil and mix well with a fork. Press the crust into a greased 13x9-inch pan. Bake for 10 minutes. Set aside.

Turn the oven down to 350°. To prepare the filling, beat together the eggs, yogurt, milk, herbs, garlic salt, and a taste of black pepper. Sauté the vegetables in a skillet in a small amount of olive oil until tender. Cool slightly and add them to the egg mixture.

Sprinkle the Feta cheese over the bottom of the prepared crust. Pour the egg–vegetable mixture over the cheese. Dust with paprika. Bake the pie for 1 hour or until the center is set.

—PEDERSON VICTORIAN B&B

Another gem of insight from Brother Juniper's Bread Book: "The intoxicating aroma of fresh-baked bread can chase the blues away.... Transcending the senses through which it reaches us, it lifts our spirits toward the good, the hopeful, and the ideal."

*E*gg Blossoms with Tomato Wine Sauce

Be sure to grease the muffin tins very well outside the molds, and, if possible, use nonstick tins so that the flower blossoms can be removed easily.

Eggs		*Sauce*	
4	sheets phyllo dough	1	pound garden-ripe tomatoes, cut into 1/2-inch dice
2	tablespoons butter, melted		
4	teaspoons freshly grated Parmesan cheese	1	clove garlic, minced
		1	small onion, minced
4	eggs	1	tablespoon white wine vinegar
4	teaspoons minced green onion	1/4	teaspoon oregano
	Salt and freshly cracked black pepper	1/2	teaspoon salt
			Oregano leaves for garnish

MAKES 4 SERVINGS

*P*reheat the oven to 350°. Arrange the phyllo leaves on a flat surface. Brush 1 sheet with melted butter and place another phyllo sheet overtop. Coat with melted butter. Slice the phyllo stack into 4x6-inch squares. Repeat with the remaining 2 sheets of phyllo.

Stack 3 squares together, rotating the squares so that the corners do not overlap. Lightly grease 4 standard muffin cups and press a stack of phyllo squares into each one. Repeat with the remaining squares. Sprinkle 1 teaspoon of cheese into each phyllo–lined cup. Then, break 1 egg into each cup and top with minced onion. Season with salt and freshly cracked black pepper. Bake for 10 to 15 minutes, or until browned.

Meanwhile, prepare the tomato sauce. Combine the tomatoes, garlic, onion, vinegar, oregano, and salt in a medium saucepan. Cook over medium heat, stirring occasionally, until the onion is tender, about 20 minutes. Serve warm over egg blossoms. Garnish with a sprig of oregano in the center of each blossom.

—THE BELVEDERE MANSION

*T*ony Femmino's Zeppole

✜

My grandmother used to make zeppole. So I have fond memories of this bread that is somewhere between a light donut and pita bread. I think you, too, will enjoy the tasty texture of innkeeper Tony Femmino's zeppole. It goes incredibly well with the inn's breakfast on page 12.

1	cup warm water
1	tablespoon yeast
2	teaspoons sugar
1	tablespoon olive oil, plus extra for frying

2	teaspoons salt
2½ to 3	cups all-purpose flour
	Powdered sugar

MAKES 8 TO 10

*I*n a large mixing bowl, whisk together the water, yeast, sugar, and olive oil. Let the mixture stand for 30 minutes. Gradually stir in the salt and flour until a sticky dough begins to form. Transfer to a lightly greased bowl and cover with a clean kitchen towel. Allow the dough to rest in a warm area, until double in size.

Knead the dough on a floured surface until smooth. Divide the dough into 2-ounce pieces and roll each into a small ball. Place 3 inches apart in a shallow dish and keep warm as before. Allow the dough to rise again, about 40 minutes.

When the dough has risen, flatten the dough balls between your palms, then roll out as thin as possible with a floured rolling pin. Heat the oil (oil should be ⅛ inch up the sides of a large skillet) on medium high heat. Drop the dough into the hot oil and cook until golden turning to cook both sides. Using tongs, turn the zeppole to brown on the reverse side. Drain on paper towels. Sprinkle with powdered sugar and serve immediately.

—A CAMBRIDGE HOUSE

Windowsill Corn Muffins
with Cilantro Mint Butter

I pranced down the stairs one morning at the Wildflower Inn to find breakfast—well—blooming on the table. Flowerpots had sprung these beautifully baked muffins and that was only the beginning. In fact, this book has other recipes sprouting from this inn, so dig in!

If you want to cook with glazed flowerpots instead of lining unglazed terra cotta pots, you may order them through Claybakers at 1-800-401-2529.

GUEST ROOMS AT THE WILDFLOWER INN MIRROR THE FLOWERS
THAT GROW THERE. THIS ONE IS CALLED THE ROSE GERANIUM ROOM.

Butter

1/2	cup butter, softened
1	tablespoon fresh minced cilantro
1	teaspoon minced peppermint or spearmint

Muffins

3/4	cup yellow cornmeal
1	cup unsifted all-purpose flour
1/4	cup sugar
2	teaspoons double-acting baking powder

1/2	teaspoon baking soda
1/2	teaspoon salt
1	cup sour cream
1/4	cup milk
1	egg, beaten
2	tablespoons butter, melted
2	tablespoons fresh minced cilantro, plus 2 tablespoons more for topping
	Garnish with rose geranium sprigs, mint, or flower petals

MAKES 6 SERVINGS

*M*ix together the butter ingredients and refrigerate. When butter is partially set, wrap with waxed paper and roll into a log. Keep cold until ready to serve.

Preheat the oven to 425°. Prepare the muffins by mixing together all the ingredients except the extra cilantro and the garnishes in a large bowl. Mix just to blend. Pour the batter into 6 greased 3-inch-wide by 2 1/2-inch-tall terra cotta flowerpots that are glazed on the inside. (Line unglazed flowerpots with aluminum foil and coat the inside of the foil with nonstick cooking spray. This bread may also be baked in an 8-inch square pan.)

Generously sprinkle more cilantro on top of the batter and let the pots rest for 10 minutes to get a good crown on the muffins. Bake in the oven for 20 minutes or until golden brown. Serve with the butter.

—THE WILDFLOWER INN

*U*sher the Southwest into your fresh tomato sauce by
adding a little lime juice, chili powder, and a few
teaspoons of diced chiles. Serve with fusilli pasta.

*H*erbed English Muffin Bread

✌◦✍

The loofa-like consistency of English muffin bread is great for breakfast spreadables. Add herbs to the bread itself; then top with lunch meats or cheeses, and you have a savory taste as homemade as days you spent at grandmother's farm. This version is easy and terrifically rewarding. Our testers suggest toasting bread slices for breakfast.

6	cups unbleached, all-purpose flour	$2^1/_2$	cups warmed milk (about 100° to 105°)
$^1/_2$	ounce active dry yeast (2 individual packages)	$^1/_2$	cup warmed water
$^1/_4$	cup sugar	2	tablespoons fresh, finely chopped basil
1	teaspoon salt	$^1/_2$	cup Parmesan cheese
$^1/_2$	teaspoon baking soda		Cornmeal for dusting

MAKES 2 LOAVES

*P*reheat the oven to 400°. In a large mixing bowl, combine 3 cups of the flour with the yeast, sugar, salt, and baking soda. Add the warm milk and water. Blend until smooth. Gradually add the remaining flour, fresh basil, and Parmesan cheese, blending well until a stiff dough forms.

Transfer the dough to a floured surface and knead for 8 minutes by hand. Divide the dough between 2 (9x5-inch) bread pans that have been sprayed with cooking oil and dusted with cornmeal. Allow the bread to rise in the pans for 45 minutes. Bake for 20 to 25 minutes or until the bread is golden on top. Remove from the pans and allow to cool on racks before cutting.

—THE CAPTAIN FREEMAN INN

LEFT: A CHERUBIC VIEW OF THE GARDEN AT SETTLERS INN

Shadows
on the
Sundial

Buckwheat and Fennel Seed Bread

~o~

The assertive flavor of buckwheat flour and the anise taste of fennel combine to make a delicious bread that is great with many cheese spreads or with melted butter.

PICTURE FACING CHAPTER OPENER: AS LUNCHTIME SETTLES IN, THE DAY GROWS OLDER, WISER, AND MORE PLENTIFUL IN THE GARDENS AT THE NOTCHLAND INN.

5	cups all-purpose flour	2	tablespoons honey
1	cup buckwheat flour	3	tablespoons active yeast
2	eggs	1	tablespoon salt
3	tablespoons fennel seeds	1³/₄	cups warm water (110°-115°)
2	tablespoons butter, softened		

MAKES 3 LOAVES

In a mixer bowl, combine all of the ingredients except 1 cup of the all-purpose flour. Mix for about 3 minutes or until the butter has melted into the dough. Add the remaining cup of flour and mix (with dough hook) on medium speed for 7 minutes. Turn the dough into a large, oil-coated bowl and allow it to rise until double in size. Punch the dough down and cut into 3 equal portions. Roll each piece into a loaf shape and place in 3 (9x5-inch) loaf pans. Allow the dough to rise again for about an hour, or until double in size. Brush the tops with a beaten egg to enhance browning. Bake at 400° for 18 to 20 minutes, or until golden brown.

—THE INN AT CEDAR FALLS

A PLACE WHERE FENNEL AND OTHER GOODIES
GROW: THE INN AT CEDAR FALLS GARDEN

Lemon Squash Soup with Orzo

While guests enjoy dinner on wooden tables outside on the inn's patio, the squash and the mint for the soup grow in a prolific garden set high on a hill overlooking the tables. Romantic.

This is an easy, refreshing soup. I have also made this without the final step of the cream and eggs, adding the lemon juice and mint while puréeing the vegetables.

1¹/₂	pounds medium yellow squash (about 3 to 4)		¹/₄	cup orzo pasta
4	tablespoons butter		¹/₂	cup light cream
1	large onion, finely minced		2	egg yolks
	Salt and freshly cracked white pepper			Juice from 1 large lemon
5	cups chicken stock		2	tablespoons finely minced fresh mint

MAKES 8 SERVINGS

Cut the squash in half lengthwise and then crosswise into ¹/₂-inch-thick slices; set aside. Melt the butter in a large soup pot over medium heat. Add the onions and cook until tender, but not browned. Add the squash and season with salt and pepper. Cover and simmer over low heat for 10 minutes. Add 4 cups of the chicken stock and bring to a boil. Reduce the heat and simmer, covered, for an additional 15 minutes, or until the squash is very soft. Remove from the heat and cool completely.

Transfer the cooled mixture to a food processor or blender. Purée until smooth. Return the soup to the pot and bring it back to a boil. Add the orzo and reduce the heat, cooking until the pasta is tender—about 7 to 8 minutes.

Meanwhile, in a separate bowl, combine the cream, egg yolks, and lemon juice. Whisk until smooth. Add the cream/egg yolk mixture to the soup and whisk over low heat until blended. Do not let the soup come to a boil, or the egg yolks will curdle. Stir in the mint.

If the soup is too thick at this point, add the remaining cup of stock. Serve immediately.

—THE INN AT CEDAR FALLS

[27]

*R*um-*Sizzled Rosemary Garden Salad Dressing*

⸱∾⸱

Nothing could be more dramatic or easier to make than this splashy dressing. The melange of citrus and herbs is almost charismatic.

After many years of trying all different types of combinations for tomato sandwiches, I finally created one that is my favorite: crusty sourdough bread brushed with extra virgin olive oil, topped with slices of vine-ripened tomatoes, sprinkled with white pepper, and topped with minced mint and cilantro.

1/4	cup dark rum
1/4	cup dry white wine
2	tablespoons brown sugar
2	tablespoons lemon juice
1/2	cup tarragon vinegar
3/4	cup corn oil
1 1/2	teaspoons minced fresh rosemary
3/4	teaspoon salt
3/4	teaspoon freshly cracked black pepper

MAKES 1 2/3 CUPS

Heat the rum in a small sauté pan. Remove from the heat and ignite with a match to burn off the alcohol. When the flames die down, allow the rum to cool to room temperature.

In a mixing bowl, combine the white wine, brown sugar, lemon juice, vinegar, corn oil, rosemary, salt, and pepper. Add the cooled rum and whisk well. Chill before serving with a salad of choice.

—THE RED HOOK INN

When buying tomato plants, buy young ones that are grown in pots and have healthy green leaves; avoid those with yellow, thin, scraggly stems.

Jícama and Pineapple Salad with Cilantro Vinaigrette

❦

Jícama is a root vegetable with a nutty flavor and is delicious raw, as in this salad, which is hard to resist. The recipe was inspired by *Bon Appétit* magazine.

THE TOOLS OF LABOR FOR GARDENS OF PLENTY

Vinaigrette

1/3	cup olive oil
3	tablespoons white wine vinegar
1	tablespoon minced shallot
1/4	cup chopped fresh cilantro
1/4	teaspoon cumin
	Salt and freshly cracked black pepper

Salad

1	6-ounce package baby spinach, stems trimmed
1	small jícama, peeled and cut julienne style, about 3/4 cup
1	cup (1/4-inch-diced) fresh pineapple
1/2	cup freshly chopped cilantro leaves

MAKES 4 SERVINGS

To prepare the vinaigrette, whisk together the oil, vinegar, shallots, chopped cilantro, and cumin. Season with salt and pepper. In a large salad bowl, combine the spinach, jícama, pineapple, and cilantro leaves. Toss the salad with enough dressing to coat. Serve immediately.

—GAIL'S KITCHEN

Make up a batch of polenta and serve it draped with your favorite fresh tomato sauce and Parmesan cheese. Add a green salad and you have lunch or dinner.

Lentil Horseradish Tart

Even her name is full of the earth's poetry. Chef Laurel Tessier created an interesting vegetarian dish full of nutrition and flavor. What a way to have some fun with lentils. The Notchland Inn serves this as an appetizer, but I am suggesting it here as a main course for lunch. Use the pre-made pie dough in the refrigerator section of the supermarket.

1	sheet pre-made pie crust dough		1	tablespoon horseradish
	Olive oil for sautéing		1	teaspoon tamari or soy sauce
1	small onion, diced		1	teaspoon cumin
1	small carrot, shredded			Salt and freshly cracked black pepper
4 to 5	mushrooms, thinly sliced		4	eggs
1	cup lentils, cooked just until tender		1/4	cup heavy cream or half-and-half

MAKES 4 TO 6 SERVINGS

*P*reheat the oven to 350°. Coat a 10-inch tart pan with cooking oil spray and line it with the pie dough. Set aside. Heat a small amount of olive oil in a medium skillet. Add the onions and cook until translucent. Add the carrots and mushrooms. Cook for a few minutes or just until crisp-tender. Reduce the heat and add the lentils. Stir in the horseradish, tamari, and cumin, adjusting the seasonings to taste.

In a mixing bowl, combine the eggs and the cream until well blended. Pour the egg/cream mixture into the skillet and then pour the entire mixture into the tart pan. Bake for 20 minutes, or until the center is set.

—THE NOTCHLAND INN

TIME OUT TO REFLECT AND PONDER AT THE NOTCHLAND INN

Couscous Vegetable and Feta Cheese Salad with Sugar Snap Peas and Chili-Lemon Dressing

❧❧❧

Serve this for lunch or as a side dish during dinner. Actually, I have eaten this as a full meal with a baby lettuce salad.

Salad

1	cup raw couscous
1½	cups boiling water (or chicken stock)
3	red bell peppers, roasted, peeled, and cut into ½-inch dice
1	pound tomatoes, cut into ½-inch dice
1	cup sugar snap peas, cut in half
½	small cucumber, peeled and cut into ½-inch dice
2	green onions, finely diced
½	cup chopped black olives
2	tablespoons parsley
1	cup crumbled Feta cheese

Dressing

¼	cup fresh lemon juice
1	teaspoon cumin
½	teaspoon chili flakes
	Salt and freshly cracked black pepper
1	clove garlic, minced
¼	cup extra virgin olive oil

MAKES 8 SERVINGS

*P*repare the salad. Place the couscous in a large saucepan and pour in the boiling liquid. Cover and allow the mixture to stand for about 20 minutes, or until cool and all of the water is absorbed. Gently toss the couscous with a fork. Add the red peppers, tomatoes, sugar snap peas, cucumber, onions, olives, parsley, and Feta cheese. Toss gently.

Prepare the dressing. Combine the lemon juice, cumin, chili flakes, salt, pepper, and garlic in a mixing bowl. Gradually whisk in the olive oil. Pour the dressing over the salad and toss well to combine.

—THE SETTLERS INN

A GUEST'S-EYE VIEW OF THE SETTLERS INN GREENHOUSE

*F*our-Grain Vegetable and Nut Salad with Maple Vinaigrette

ನಿ⌒ನಿ

The eclectic mixture of mustard, balsamic vinegar, and maple syrup will please most palates. Pour over a salad with mandarin oranges or any green salad with fruit. You need to start preparing the dish a day ahead of time in order to tenderize the grains.

THE SETTLERS INN'S POTTING SHED

Salad

¹/₂	cup whole-wheat berries
¹/₄	cup whole spelt
¹/₄	cup barley
¹/₂	cup wild rice
¹/₂	red bell pepper, finely diced
¹/₂	yellow bell pepper, finely diced
1	tablespoon olive oil
1	tablespoon balsamic vinegar
¹/₂	bunch scallions with green tops, finely diced
¹/₂	cup fresh corn kernels, blanched
¹/₄	cup toasted almonds (or pine nuts)
8	shiitake mushrooms, caps only, thinly sliced

Vinaigrette

4	tablespoons balsamic vinegar
4	tablespoons olive oil
¹/₄	teaspoon salt
¹/₄	teaspoon freshly cracked black pepper
3	tablespoons maple syrup
1	tablespoon Dijon-style mustard

MAKES 8 SERVINGS

*P*lace the whole-wheat berries, spelt, barley, and rice in a large bowl with water 2 inches above the grains. Cover and soak overnight. Drain and transfer the grains to a large saucepan. Add 3 cups of salted water and cook over medium–high heat until al dente, about 10 to 15 minutes. Drain and transfer to a large mixing bowl.

Preheat the oven to 350°. Place the diced red and yellow peppers in a shallow baking dish with the olive oil and balsamic vinegar. Bake for about 8 minutes. Add the peppers to the grains along with the scallions, corn, toasted nuts, and the sliced mushroom caps. Toss well and set aside.

In a separate bowl, combine all the vinaigrette ingredients. Whisk well and toss with the grain salad. Chill awhile or serve immediately.

—THE SETTLERS INN

Fireflies
and
Candlelight

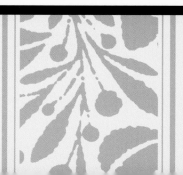

Garden Bruschetta with Basil Oil

✌️◦✍

Chef Abby Freethy's recipe has all of the ingredients I love in an appetizer—basil, goat cheese, little yellow tomatoes, and fresh edible flowers. The vitamin C provides the infused oil with citric acid to preserve the color of the basil. Prepare this recipe a day ahead.

If you ever get the chance, stop by a cornfield after sunset and you can hear the corn growing. That muffled, cracking sound is the ears of corn pushing through the stalks; the husks reaching out toward the sky.

PICTURE FACING CHAPTER OPENER: WINDING DOWN AND REAPING THE DAY'S REWARDS AT THE WILDFLOWER INN

Basil Oil

1	cup extra virgin olive oil
3	tablespoons finely chopped fresh basil
1	vitamin C tablet

Bruschetta

1	loaf thick-crusted bread, cut into $^1/_2$ to $^3/_4$-inch slices
1	12-ounce log goat cheese

$^1/_2$	pint yellow pear tomatoes, coarsely chopped
$^1/_4$	cup finely chopped fresh herbs (such as parsley, thyme, and sage)
15	flower petals (such as pansy, nasturtium, and rose petals), cleaned
2	tablespoons raspberry vinegar

MAKES 8 TO 10 SERVINGS

Prepare the basil oil. In a food processor or blender, process the oil, basil, and vitamin C tablet for 30 seconds. Strain the mixture through a fine mesh cloth. Refrigerate overnight so the flavors intensify.

Prepare the bruschetta. Grill or broil the bread slices on both sides until golden brown. Arrange the bread on a platter and brush one side with basil oil.

In a mixing bowl, combine the goat cheese, yellow pear tomatoes, and half of the fresh herbs. Sprinkle evenly on the oiled bread slices.

In a separate bowl, gently toss the flower petals with the raspberry vinegar. Arrange the flowers over the goat cheese mixture to top off the bruschetta. Garnish with the remaining chopped herbs.

—THE INN AT MEADOWBROOK

Country Corn and Crab Soup

✼

Simple and elegant, this soup may be made with or without the crab meat and with light cream instead of heavy. It is a velvety soup with a slightly earthy taste thanks to the fresh corn kernels. Instead of adding the crab to the bowl you may add whole kernels of corn. Our testers also enjoyed this with 3 tablespoons of sherry added to the recipe.

IN THE GARDENS OF THE INN AT MEADOWBROOK

24	ears of corn, kernels cut off (or 24 ounces frozen corn kernels)
1	large yellow onion, peeled and sliced
4	cups chicken or vegetable stock
1	cup heavy cream
	Salt and freshly cracked white pepper
1	pound jumbo lump crab meat
	Fresh sage leaves

MAKES 8 TO 10 SERVINGS

In a large stockpot, combine the corn, onion, and stock. Simmer for about 30 minutes. Purée the corn mixture in a blender—2 cups at a time. Strain and return the liquid to the stockpot. Simmer for another 10 minutes. Stir in the cream and season with salt and freshly cracked white pepper.

To serve, place a generous amount of crab meat in the bottom of each soup bowl. Ladle the hot corn soup overtop. Garnish with fresh sage.

—THE INN AT MEADOWBROOK

PEACEFUL GARDENS AND TRANQUIL SPLENDOR ARE THE HALLMARKS OF THE INN AT MEADOWBROOK IN EAST STROUDSBURG, PENNSYLVANIA.

Light Garden Minestrone Soup

Not your usual minestrone, this soup is a lighter version made without beans and pasta and only fresh herbs and vegetables from the garden. Believe me, it will become one of your all-time favorite recipes.

A first-rate soup is more creative than a second-rate painting.
—*Abraham Maslow*

1 to 2	tablespoons olive oil		1	zucchini, thinly sliced
1	leek (white part only), cut into 1/4-inch dice		1	yellow squash, thinly sliced
1	rib celery, finely diced		1	tablespoon finely chopped fresh marjoram
1	carrot, peeled and cut into 1/2-inch dice		1	tablespoon finely chopped fresh basil
1	clove garlic, minced		1	teaspoon finely chopped fresh thyme
1	green bell pepper, cut into 1/2-inch dice			Salt and freshly cracked black pepper
6	plum tomatoes, seeded and coarsely chopped			Freshly grated Parmesan cheese
6	cups chicken or vegetable stock			
1/4	pound green beans, snapped into 1-inch pieces			

MAKES 6 TO 8 SERVINGS

*H*eat the olive oil in a large skillet. Sauté the leek, celery, and carrot for 5 minutes, or until tender. Add the garlic and green pepper; sauté for an additional 2 minutes. Add the tomatoes and cook just until the juices are released. Pour in the stock and bring the mixture to a boil. Reduce the heat and simmer for 10 minutes. Return to a boil and add the green beans, zucchini, and squash. Lower the heat to a simmer and cook until the vegetables are just crisp/tender. Stir in the marjoram, basil, and thyme; and garnish with freshly grated Parmesan cheese. Serve immediately.

—OCTOBER COUNTRY INN

ABOVE: WHAT'S BURNT ORANGE AND BLACK, AND SMILES AT YOU IN ANY SEASON? THE OCTOBER COUNTRY INN.

Stuffed Bell Peppers with Vegetables and Tofu

✎

Served as an appetizer at the inn, this dish is suggested here as a main course with a garden salad for those who prefer a meatless meal.

2	large red bell peppers		¹/₂	pound tofu, finely chopped
	Olive oil for sautéing		2	Roma tomatoes, diced
1	large onion, finely diced		2	teaspoons tamari or soy sauce
3	cloves garlic, minced			Salt and freshly cracked black pepper
1	small bunch basil, finely chopped		¹/₂	cup dry white wine

MAKES 2 SERVINGS

*R*emove the tops of the peppers and scoop out the seeds. Rinse and set aside, reserving the tops.

Preheat the oven to 350°. In a medium sauté pan, heat a small amount of olive oil. Add the onion, and cook, covered, until soft and translucent. Add the garlic, basil, tofu, and tomatoes. Sauté until the ingredients are heated through. Stir in the tamari and season with salt and pepper. Arrange the peppers on a well-greased pie plate. Fill each cavity with the tofu mixture. Pour white wine over the vegetables and replace the pepper top. Bake for about 15 minutes, or until the pepper is tender.

—THE NOTCHLAND INN

Salmon with Dill Lemon Sauce

~o~

Salmon is such a versatile fish and this sauce complements the pure clean taste of the fish with a touch of nature above water. Serve this with a side of orzo pasta and sugar snap peas.

3	slices white bread, cut into small pieces	2	teaspoons Dijon-style mustard
2	tablespoons fresh lemon juice	1/2	teaspoon grated lemon peel
3	tablespoons water	1/8	teaspoon sugar
3/4	cup finely chopped fresh dill	1/3	cup olive oil
3/4	cup finely chopped flat-leaf parsley	1	3-pound salmon filet

MAKES 6 SERVINGS

*P*reheat the oven to 400°. Soak the bread pieces in lemon juice and water for 10 minutes. Squeeze out the excess liquid and place the bread in a food processor bowl. Add the dill, parsley, mustard, lemon peel, sugar, and olive oil. Process until the mixture forms a paste.

Slice the salmon into 6 steaks. Sauté the salmon in a small amount of oil for three minutes on each side. Transfer the filets to the oven and bake for about 5 to 8 minutes until done.

Spread a dollop of the dill lemon sauce on each salmon filet and serve extra on the side. Note: If the sauce is too thick, it may be thinned with 2 tablespoons of hot water.

—OCTOBER COUNTRY INN

October Country Inn likes to season its green beans by blending over medium heat 3 tablespoons butter with a teaspoon of grated lemon peel, a tablespoon of minced fresh rosemary, and a taste of salt and pepper. Add cooked beans and blend with the sauce.

Chicken Flowerpot Pies

The dough needs to chill 3 hours ahead of prep time. Terra cotta flowerpots are usually safe to cook in if glazed. (See page 18 for a company that makes them.) Otherwise, if using unglazed pots, be sure that you line the pots as described below. (The recipe may also be made with a 9-inch, deep-dish pie crust and baked according to the same method.)

Pie Dough

2	cups all-purpose flour
1	teaspoon salt
3/4	cup (1 1/2 sticks) butter, chilled
3	tablespoons vegetable shortening
1/2	cup ice water

Filling

2	cups chicken broth
1/2	cup dry sherry
1 1/2	cups green beans, cut into 1-inch lengths
1 1/2	cups sliced carrots, cut into 1/4-inch-thick rounds
1	cup diced potato, peeled and cut into 1/2-inch cubes
1	teaspoon dried basil
1	teaspoon dried thyme
3/4	cup quartered mushrooms of choice

1	10-ounce package frozen peas
1	16-ounce can whole, peeled plum tomatoes, drained and quartered
3 1/2	cups shredded, cooked chicken, set aside

Sauce

1/4	cup (1/2 stick) butter
1/4	cup all-purpose flour
1	cup heavy cream
2	egg yolks
	Salt and pepper

Assembly

6	4 x 4-inch ovenproof flowerpots
6	12-inch squares of aluminum foil
	Cooking oil spray
	Egg wash made of 1 egg yolk mixed with 1 tablespoon water

*P*repare pie dough. Place flour and salt into a large mixing bowl. Cut butter in thin slices; mix with shortening into the flour, using a pastry blender or 2 knives; until coarse crumbs form. Sprinkle the ice water evenly overtop; mix rapidly with a fork. Gather the dough into a ball and refrigerate for 3 hours or overnight.

Prepare the filling. When ready to prepare the pies, heat the broth and sherry in a medium saucepan. Add green beans, carrots, potatoes, basil, and thyme. Cover the pot and cook on medium-low heat for 12 to 15 minutes or until the vegetables are just tender. Add the mushrooms, peas, and tomatoes. Cover and simmer for 2 to 4 minutes. Drain the vegetables, reserving the liquid. (There should be 1½ cups of broth; add water if necessary.) Set aside.

Prepare the sauce. In a Dutch oven, melt the butter and whisk in the ¼ cup flour. Whisk in reserved broth. Cook over low heat, stirring constantly, until sauce is smooth and thick. Set aside.

In a small bowl, beat the cream and egg yolks; beat into the sauce and remove from heat. Add salt and pepper to taste. Fold in the chicken and cooked vegetables. Cool to room temperature.

Preheat the oven to 425°. Prepare pie crusts. Remove the dough from the refrigerator; set aside. Turn each flowerpot upside-down and shape a swatch of foil around the outside from

bottom to top of pot. Remove the foil intact; turn pot right-side up, placing foil inside without tearing. Trim excess foil; foil should just reach the top.

Spray linings with nonstick coating. Spoon pie filling evenly into the pots to within ½ inch of the top. Roll the dough out to ⅛-inch thickness; cut into 6 (6-inch) circles. Place a circle of dough over each pot; carefully mold dough around the top of the pot; crimp the edges; pierce crust for 3 or 4 steam holes.

Brush the top of each crust with egg wash. Place pots on baking sheets and bake for 35 to 40 minutes or until heated through and crust is golden brown.

Place flowerpots in baskets with homemade biscuits, cloth napkin, lunch plate, new mini-garden spade, and eating fork; or serve in the center of a luncheon-size plate.

—GAIL'S KITCHEN

Rhubarb and Walnut Bread

❦

October Country Inn Chef Patrick Runkel waxes sentimental about this bread. He had rhubarb growing in the backyard when he was a boy; so his mother made this bread very often. It is moist, tasty, and a good way to use up garden rhubarb.

Bread

1¹/₂	cups packed brown sugar
²/₃	cup vegetable oil
1	egg
1	cup buttermilk or sour milk (pour 1 tablespoon lemon juice into a measuring cup; add milk to measure 1 cup and let sit for 3 minutes)
1	teaspoon salt

1	teaspoon baking soda
1	teaspoon vanilla extract
2¹/₂	cups all-purpose flour
1¹/₂	cups finely diced rhubarb
¹/₂	cup coarsely chopped walnuts

Topping

1	tablespoon butter, at room temperature
¹/₂	cup sugar

MAKES 1 LOAF

Preheat the oven to 325°. Prepare the bread. In a large mixing bowl, stir together the bread ingredients in the order given. Divide the batter in half, and pour into 2 greased and floured 9x5-inch loaf pans—about ²/₃ full.

Prepare the topping. Cream the butter and sugar together until smooth. Sprinkle the mixture over each loaf. Bake for 40 minutes, or until tester comes clean.

—OCTOBER COUNTRY INN

LEFT: COOLING DOWN ON A SUMMER'S DAY: THE RHUBARB AND WALNUT BREAD ON THE PORCH AT OCTOBER COUNTRY INN

Chocolate Garden Beet Cake
with Vanilla Sauce

✧

I really enjoy beets freshly pulled from the garden. The flavor of the sweet beets and the chocolate is accented by the plain but sweet vanilla sauce. People will be surprised when you tell them that this is a cake made with beets. Cook the beets in boiling water until tender. Remove the skins and chop coarsely. Purée just enough to blend (they should still be a bit lumpy).

1³/₄	cups unsifted all-purpose flour		*Sauce*	
1¹/₂	teaspoons baking powder		¹/₄	cup sugar
¹/₂	teaspoon salt		1	tablespoon cornstarch
3	eggs		1	cup water
1¹/₂	cups sugar		2	tablespoons butter
1	cup canola oil		¹/₈	teaspoon salt
1¹/₂	cups freshly cooked beets, puréed		2	tablespoons vanilla extract, or rum (or rum extract)
2	1-ounce squares unsweetened chocolate, melted		*Assembly*	
1	teaspoon vanilla extract			Beets diced finely for garnish
				Whipped cream for garnish

MAKES 6 TO 8 SERVINGS

*P*reheat the oven to 375°. In a large bowl, combine the flour, baking powder, and salt. Set aside.

In a separate bowl, beat the eggs, gradually adding in the sugar. When the mixture is well blended, add the oil, beets, and chocolate. Mix well. Slowly add the dry ingredients, beating until thoroughly combined. Stir in the vanilla extract. Turn the batter into a greased 13x9-inch pan. Bake for 25 to 30 minutes, or until a tester comes clean. Allow cake to cool to room temperature.

Meanwhile prepare the sauce. In a double boiler over hot but not boiling water,

combine the sugar, cornstarch, and water until thickened. Remove from the heat. Stir in the butter, salt, and vanilla extract or rum. Pool the sauce in the bottom of the dessert dishes. Cut the cake into squares (about 3 inches) and place in the middle of the pooled sauce. Serve garnished with diced beets and some whipped cream.

—GAIL'S KITCHEN

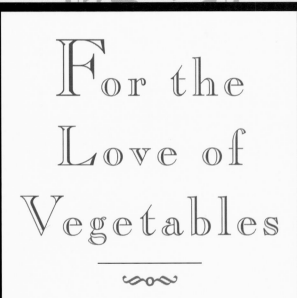

For the
Love of
Vegetables

Spaghetti Garden Ragout

࿇

A quick sauté of tomatoes, zucchini, and onions, combined with melted Mozzarella tops spaghetti al dente. Serve with a glass of dry white wine. Our testers were simply mad about this recipe and used plum tomatoes; whole canned tomatoes otherwise.

Plant cool-weather crops such as beets, broccoli, cabbage, carrots, lettuce, onions, peas, potatoes, spinach, and radishes, one month before the last predicted spring frost.

PICTURE FACING CHAPTER OPENER: LIKE SOMETHING OUT OF A THORNTON WILDER PLAY, OCTOBER COUNTRY INN PROVIDES A LOOK AT THE PAST.

1½	tablespoons olive oil		¼	teaspoon fresh oregano
1	large clove garlic, minced		⅛	teaspoon freshly cracked black pepper
2	medium zucchini, thinly sliced and halved lengthwise		1	cup shredded Mozzarella cheese
1	large onion, sliced into thin rings		½	pound thin spaghetti, cooked
2	medium tomatoes, seeded and quartered		2	tablespoons butter
¼	teaspoon salt		¼	cup grated Asiago or Parmesan cheese
¼	teaspoon minced basil leaves			

MAKES 2 SERVINGS

*H*eat the olive oil in a large skillet. Add the minced garlic and sauté until the garlic just begins to brown. Add the zucchini and onion and continue to sauté over medium heat until tender. Add the tomatoes, salt, basil, oregano, and pepper. Cover and simmer for 3 to 5 minutes.

Remove the pan from the heat and sprinkle with Mozzarella cheese. Cover and allow the dish to sit for 3 to 4 minutes, or until the cheese melts.

Meanwhile, toss the spaghetti with the butter and cheese. Arrange the pasta on a large platter and top with the warm vegetables. Serve immediately.

—MAST FARM INN

*P*lant warm-weather crops such as beans, corn, cucumbers, peppers, tomatoes, and squash, only once the danger of frost is over.

Fiddleheads and Fettuccine

You'll hear the strains of violins while eating this dish. Fiddlehead ferns and fettuccine go hand-in-hand. The vegetable's tightly coiled top resembles the spiral end of a violin with the pasta—well—serving as the string section? Rich in vitamins A and C, choose fiddleheads that are bright green and firm. They grow wild at Inn at Maplewood Farm and in many places throughout New England. You may find fiddlehead fern bottled at gourmet shops or substitute with chopped fresh green beans.

A COOLING RESPITE ON THE PORCH AFTER PICKING FIDDLE-HEAD FERNS AT THE INN AT MAPLEWOOD FARM

1	pound fettuccine or linguine			Salt and freshly cracked black pepper
2	pounds fiddlehead ferns		4	slices bacon, cooked and crumbled
1/2	cup unsalted butter			
2	tablespoons minced garlic		1/2	cup freshly grated Romano cheese
2	tablespoons minced shallots			

MAKES 4 SERVINGS

*P*repare pasta. *Cook the pasta until al dente. Drain and set aside.*
Prepare fern mixture. Pick over the ferns, removing the paperlike brown mem-

branes. Trim the stems. Place the ferns in a large pot of boiling water and blanch for 1 minute. Drain and rinse under cold water.

In a large skillet, melt the butter over medium-high heat. Add the garlic and shallots and sauté for 20 to 30 seconds, or until just aromatic. Add the fiddleheads and cook for 2 minutes. Season with salt and pepper. Divide the fettuccine among 4 individual serving plates. Top the pasta with the sautéed fiddleheads, a bit of crumbled bacon, and a sprinkling of Romano cheese.

—THE INN AT MAPLEWOOD FARM

ORCHESTRATING DINNER WITH A NEW ENGLAND WILD VEGETABLE: THE FIDDLEHEAD FERN

Vegetable Stroganoff

✎

A creamy but low-fat, spicy sauce with a dash of garden-pulled dill mixed with fresh vegetables over shimmering egg noodles, offers a vegetarian version of the traditional meat-style stroganoff.

Asparagus and rhubarb are great crops for a home garden, because they are perennials; so every year they provide a bountiful reward.

2	tablespoons butter		3 to 4	drops tamari or soy sauce
1	cup finely chopped yellow onion		$1/8$	teaspoon paprika
				Freshly cracked black pepper
$1/2$	pound wild mushrooms, chopped		6	cups ($1/2$-inch diced) assorted fresh vegetables (such as artichokes, broccoli, carrots, zucchini, celery, cabbage, bell peppers, and cherry tomatoes)
3	cups sour cream			
$1\frac{1}{2}$	cups plain yogurt			
3	tablespoons dry red wine		1	pound wide egg noodles
$3/4$	teaspoon salt			
$1/4$	teaspoon fresh chopped dill weed			

MAKES 6 SERVINGS

*M*ake *the stroganoff sauce. Melt the butter in a large skillet. Sauté the onions and mushrooms until tender. Transfer the mixture to the top of a double boiler and add the sour cream, yogurt and red wine. Season with salt, dill, tamari sauce, paprika, and pepper. Cook gently on low for about 30 minutes.*

Meanwhile, steam the vegetables until tender. Cook the egg noodles in boiling water. Drain and set aside.

To serve, arrange the noodles on a large serving platter. Top with steamed vegetables and stroganoff sauce.

—THE INN AT CEDAR FALLS

Back of the Beyond, a B&B in Colden, New York, offers this for spreading the garden on an English muffin: Mix grated Mozzarella and Parmesan with just enough mayonnaise to bind. Drop in Tabasco to taste, minced scallions, and finely diced green peppers. Finish with dill, marjoram, and thyme. Spread on muffins and broil.

Roasted Vegetable Galette

༶ঙ৹

Hailing from medieval France, a *galette* usually refers to a cake made of flaky peasant pastry dough, but it also applies to a variety of savory and sweet tarts. This one is gathered up like a bundle with some of the vegetables showing through an opening in the center. A galette is somewhere between a tart and a pizza. I use the prepared pastry dough sheets in the dairy section of the supermarket.

1	medium eggplant, sliced into 1/4-inch-thick pieces		Salt and freshly cracked black pepper
4	large cremini mushrooms, caps only, sliced 1/4-inch thick	4	ounces herbed goat cheese, crumbled
2	medium shallots, thinly sliced	3	ounces cream cheese, softened
1	medium red bell pepper, cut into 1/2-inch dice	1	egg
1	medium zucchini, sliced crosswise 1/4-inch thick	1	tablespoon freshly grated Asiago cheese
2	tablespoons olive oil	2	sheets prepared pie crusts
			Egg wash

MAKES 6 SERVINGS

*P*reheat the oven to 450°. Line 2 baking sheets with foil or use nonstick baking sheets.

Prepare the cheese mixture. In a large roasting pan, toss the eggplant, mushrooms, shallots, red pepper, and zucchini with the olive oil, salt, and pepper. Roast the vegetables for 12 to 14 minutes, stirring once or twice, until tender.

In a mixing bowl, beat the goat cheese and cream cheese together until smooth. Add the egg and the Asiago cheese; continue beating until the mixture is well-blended.

Prepare the pastry. Roll the pastry sheets out to 1/8-inch thickness. Arrange 1 pie crust on each baking sheet.

Assemble the galettes. *Spread the cheese mixture on each crust, leaving a 2-inch border of dough. Place the roasted vegetables on top. Fold the dough to partially cover the filling, crimping to seal the edges. Brush the dough with egg wash. Bake in the same oven for 20 to 25 minutes or until golden brown.*

—GAIL'S KITCHEN

[65]

*T*uscan Bean and Vegetable Soup

✺

One night my aunt invited me over for a spur-of-the-moment dinner. She apologized that she had made only a simple Italian bean soup. But I was so excited, I couldn't contain myself. We ate until every bit was gone, sipping wine in between spoonfuls of soup and bites of Italian bread. Sometimes the very simplest dishes are the best; like this one with the Italian garden in mind.

The Inn at Maplewood Farm gives zip to green beans. In a medium skillet, sauté until soft: a clove of pressed garlic with a 1/2-inch slice of ginger, a sliced green onion, and 2 teaspoons olive oil. Add a pound of trimmed green beans and a teaspoon soy sauce. Simmer 10 minutes until tender.

1/2	pound small navy beans	1	pound savoy cabbage, shredded
6 to 7	cups vegetable (or beef) stock		
1	tablespoon olive oil	2	tablespoons tomato paste
2	ounces prosciutto, chopped	1/4	teaspoon crushed red pepper flakes
1/4	cup chopped Italian parsley		
1	clove garlic, minced	1	bay leaf
1	large carrot, coarsely chopped	1/4	cup long-grain rice
1	large onion, coarsely chopped		Freshly grated Parmesan cheese
1	fennel bulb, coarsely chopped		

MAKES 6 SERVINGS

In a large soup pot, combine the beans and the stock. Bring to a boil. Reduce the heat and simmer for 1 hour and 15 minutes, or until the beans are tender.

Meanwhile, heat the olive oil in a large skillet. Add the prosciutto, parsley, and garlic. Sauté for about 5 minutes, stirring frequently. Add the carrots, onions, and fennel, and continue to sauté, stirring often, for an additional 10 minutes. Add the cabbage, tomato paste, and crushed red peppers. Cook for another 5 minutes.

Transfer the sautéed vegetable mixture to the kettle. Make sure there is enough stock to cover the vegetables. Add more as needed. Add the bay leaf and bring the soup to a boil. Then, using a wooden spoon, stir in the rice. Cover and reduce the heat to medium low. Cook for 15 minutes, stirring often.

To serve, remove the bay leaf and garnish individual soup bowls with grated Parmesan cheese.

—THE INN AT ORMSBY HILL

ABOVE: THE INN AT ORMSBY HILL IN MANCHESTER, VERMONT

*V*idalia and Rhubarb Ratatouille

~o~

At the inn, this relish is served with a grilled Tuscan-style chicken. The ratatouille could accompany fish as well.

1/4	cup extra virgin olive oil		1/4	cup balsamic vinegar
2	large Vidalia onions, thinly sliced		1 1/2	pounds rhubarb, cut into 1-inch pieces
3	large tomatoes, peeled, seeded, and chopped		1 1/2	pounds red bell peppers, roasted, peeled and sliced into strips
1/3	cup light brown sugar			
1	teaspoon coriander seeds, coarsely ground		1	tablespoon drained capers, coarsely chopped
1/3	cup mustard seeds, coarsely ground			Salt and freshly cracked black pepper

MAKES 6 TO 8 SERVINGS

*H*eat the olive oil in a large skillet over low heat. Add the onions and cook until tender. Add the tomatoes, sugar, coriander seeds, mustard seeds, and vinegar. Sauté over medium heat for 5 minutes. Add the rhubarb and peppers, and cook until just soft. Stir in the capers, salt, and pepper, and serve.

—THE BELMONT INN

Sugar snap peas (1 pound) go great with a mixture of 2 tablespoons soft butter, 1/2 teaspoon lemon juice, and 2 teaspoons minced fresh lemon thyme.

LEFT: ONE OF LIFE'S SIMPLE PLEASURES: RIDING THROUGH THE COUNTRYSIDE TO FETCH FRESH FLOWERS AND BAKED BREAD FOR THE TABLE, À LA THE INN AT MEADOWBROOK.

Savory Tomato Cobbler

∽o∾

A homemade biscuit topping provides the crust for a filling of vine-ripened tomatoes and sautéed onions. Savory cobblers are akin to pot pies and were popular in Colonial America. This one was inspired by *Charles Wysocki's Americana Cookbook*.

My favorite tomato chutney is from the Old Drover's Inn in Dover Plains, New York: Combine 2 cups medium-diced ripe tomatoes with 1 cup sugar and a bouquet garni of cloves and cinnamon sticks; simmer uncovered over medium-low heat for 3 hours or until liquid has almost evaporated. Stir with a wooden spoon to prevent sticking. Delicious with meats or serve with cream cheese and crackers.

Filling		Biscuit Topping	
4	tablespoons unsalted butter	1/2	cup stone-ground yellow cornmeal
1/4	cup finely chopped green onion	1 1/2	cups unbleached all-purpose flour
1	rib celery, minced	2 1/2	teaspoons baking powder
2	pounds vine-ripened tomatoes (about 6 medium tomatoes)	1/2	teaspoon baking soda
1	teaspoon fresh sage	1/2	teaspoon salt
1	teaspoon fresh oregano	3	tablespoons cold, unsalted butter
1	teaspoon sugar	3	tablespoons chilled vegetable shortening
1/4	teaspoon salt	3/4	cup buttermilk
	Freshly cracked black pepper		

MAKES 6 TO 8 SERVINGS

*P*repare the filling. Preheat the oven to 400°. Melt the butter in a large skillet over medium heat. Add the onion and celery and cook until the celery is tender.

Peel the tomatoes by blanching them in boiling water for about 15 seconds. Drain, peel, and core the tomatoes. Cut into quarters. Stir the tomatoes into the onion-celery mixture. Add the sage and oregano. Season with sugar, salt, and pepper. Mix well. Pour the mixture into an 8-inch square casserole dish. Set aside.

Prepare the biscuit topping. Combine the cornmeal, flour, baking powder, soda, and salt in a food processor. Whirl briefly until blended. Cut the butter and shortening into small pieces and add them to the processor. Pulse quickly until coarse crumbs form. Transfer the mixture to a large bowl. Add the buttermilk, stirring until a dough begins to form. Place the dough on a lightly floured surface and knead until smooth. Roll out to about 1/2-inch thick. Using a 2-inch biscuit cutter, press out rounds until all the dough is used. Arrange the biscuits on top of the tomatoes in the casserole.

Bake for 20 minutes, or until the biscuit topping is lightly browned.

— GAIL'S KITCHEN

Much A-Dew about Herbs

Herbs in 4-inch pots on the breakfast table complement the morning meal and help you open your eyes faster as you inhale their motivating scents.

*B*asil Soup

∽o∾

Leave it to the Inn at Cedar Falls to come up with a basil soup. The garden grows quite prolifically here, and the chef and the innkeeper thrive on developing and changing their dishes constantly. I like having this recipe because it uses up a lot of basil, helping to put this abundantly growing herb to good use.

3	tablespoons butter	6	tablespoons white or brown rice
3/4	cup finely chopped scallions		
1	clove garlic, minced	3 1/2	cups chopped fresh basil (or 1 1/2 tablespoons dried basil)
4	cups chicken or vegetable stock		
2	medium tomatoes, peeled, seeded, and chopped		

MAKES 8 SERVINGS

*M*elt the butter in a heavy saucepan. Add the scallions and the garlic and sauté until tender. Add the stock, tomatoes, and rice. Cover and simmer for 25 minutes over low heat. Stir in the basil and simmer for an additional 10 minutes. Serve immediately.

—THE INN AT CEDAR FALLS

Flat-bottom ice cream cones can be small vases (no water) for freshly snipped herbs or hearty flowers. The cones are small enough so that each place setting has its own flowers.

Fresh Mint and Pea Soup

༄

I like any excuse to use mint in a recipe. I sprinkle it into salads, morning fruit smoothies, and some sweet breads, not to mention many seafood and chicken entrées.

Throw whole sprigs of herbs onto the coals when grilling. The herbal smoke flavors whatever you're cooking. Add whole sprigs to sauces, soups, and stews while they simmer on the stove; then remove before serving.

3	whole leeks, cleaned and finely chopped	2	cups freshly shelled peas (or 2 cups tiny frozen peas)
1	medium onion, minced		Salt and freshly cracked black pepper
2	tablespoons butter		
5	cups vegetable or chicken stock	1	cup light cream
			Yogurt or sour cream, mint leaves for garnish
1	cup (about 2 handfuls) fresh mint leaves, coarsely chopped		

MAKES 6 TO 8 SERVINGS

In a heavy saucepan, sauté the leeks and onion in the butter until tender, about 5 to 6 minutes. Stir in the stock and bring to a boil. Add the chopped mint leaves and peas. If you are using frozen peas, remove the pan from the heat and let cool. If using fresh peas, reduce the heat and simmer for 2 to 5 minutes, or until tender.

Transfer the soup to a blender and purée until smooth. Return to the saucepan to heat. Season with salt and pepper. Stir in the cream just before serving. Garnish with yogurt or sour cream and top with fresh mint sprigs.

—HARBOR HOUSE INN BY THE SEA

Lemon balm butter is great with chicken or seafood or just slathered on savory scones or French bread. Here is a recipe from the Notchland Inn: Combine 2 sticks soft unsalted butter with 1/4 cup chopped lemon balm. In a saucepan, boil 1/4 cup white wine with 1 small diced onion. Lower heat and cook until wine evaporates. Cool. Stir onion into the butter. Season with salt, pepper, and a teaspoon lemon juice. Chill and serve.

Smoked Chicken and Sage Pinwheels

‿〜◦〜‿

The musky scent and taste of the sage with the mild flavor of Derby Sage cheese and the piquant apricot jam, all folded into a sheet of puff pastry, make up this impressive appetizer. If you cannot find the cheese, substitute with mild Cheddar cheese or plain Derby cheese.

1	large sheet puff pastry		4	ounces smoked chicken, finely chopped
2	tablespoons apricot jam		2	ounces Derby Sage cheese
12	sage leaves			

MAKES 12 PINWHEELS

Preheat the oven to 400°. Place the puff pastry sheet on a flat surface. Brush the sheet with a thin layer of apricot jam. Top the pastry with the sage leaves. Add smoked chicken and cheese, distributing evenly. Roll the pastry up jellyroll style and slice at 1/2-inch intervals. Arrange the pinwheel slices, stuffing side up, on 2 well-greased baking sheets. Bake for about 20 minutes, or until brown and puffy.

—THE NOTCHLAND INN

My grandmother served fennel as a palate cleanser. Separate the celery-like stalks and serve them on a plate with a cherry tomato garnish. Let everyone help themselves during the course of a meal, eating the white part and leaving the stem. Cooking fennel mutes its anise flavor, but eating it raw, offers a clean, fresh taste.

Herb-Crusted Pork with Apricot Sauce

In this recipe, you make an herbal paste that is rubbed into the pork. A chunky sweet sauce accompanies the pork.

Pork			1	pork tenderloin (3 to 4 pounds)
1/4	cup mixture sage, rosemary, mint, lemon balm, marjoram, and thyme			
		Sauce		
1	tablespoon stone-ground mustard		3/4	cup dried apricots (softened in boiling water)
1	tablespoon extra virgin olive oil		2	teaspoons lemon juice
			1	teaspoon tamari or soy sauce
2	teaspoons balsamic vinegar		1/8	teaspoon cinnamon
	Salt and freshly cracked black pepper		1/8	teaspoon kosher salt
1/8	teaspoon sugar (optional)			

MAKES 6 TO 8 SERVINGS

*P*reheat the oven to 450°. Prepare the pork. In a food processor, combine the herbs, mustard, olive oil, vinegar, salt, pepper, and sugar. Mix until a paste forms. Rub the herb paste into the pork tenderloin, making sure to distribute evenly. Place the pork in the preheated oven for 10 minutes. Reduce the heat to 350° and cook for about 1 hour, or until a meat thermometer reads 160°. Allow the pork to rest for 10 minutes before carving.

Meanwhile, prepare the apricot purée. Place the apricots in a metal mixing bowl and add enough boiling water to cover. Soak until the fruit has softened. Transfer the apricots to a food processor (reserving the water) and blend until smooth. Stir in the lemon juice, soy sauce, cinnamon, and salt. Add some of the water to thin consistency, if desired. Serve warm with herbed pork.

—THE NOTCHLAND INN

*T*o prepare fennel for cooking, remove its wilted outer layers and cut and discard a slice from the base. Cut off the tough upper stalks and feathery fronds, leaving the tender bulb for cooking. Or, just grate fennel julienne style and serve on top of a salad.

Bow Ties Vegetarian with Walnut Pesto

᠃᠃

Orange carrots, green squash, textured nuts, and the lacy look of delicate herbs make for a joyous plate to set before a guest. I like this twist on basil paste. Here, a medley of herbs with walnuts, instead of pine nuts, provides the sauce.

1	cup packed flat-leaf parsley	1/3	cup olive oil
1/2	cup finely chopped fresh basil leaves, packed	1/4	cup chopped walnuts, toasted
1	tablespoon fresh thyme leaves	1	tablespoon balsamic vinegar
1	tablespoon fresh rosemary leaves		Salt and freshly cracked black pepper
1	tablespoon fresh tarragon leaves	1	pound bow-tie pasta
		2	carrots, cut julienne style
1/2	cup Parmesan cheese	1	zucchini, cut julienne style

MAKES 6 TO 8 SERVINGS

Place the herbs, Parmesan cheese, olive oil, walnuts, vinegar, salt, and pepper in a food processor. Blend until a paste forms.

Cook the pasta in a large pot of boiling water. About 3 minutes before the pasta is done, add the vegetables. Reserve 2/3 cup of the pasta water and drain. Toss the pasta and vegetables with herb pesto and the reserved water. Serve immediately.

—OCTOBER COUNTRY INN

Here's a recipe from the Nuthatch B&B for herbal-garlic spread that may be used for so many preparations from omelets to baked tomatoes or simply bread or crackers: Process a garlic clove with 1/2 pound Feta cheese. Add 1/2 cup mayonnaise and a teaspoon each of fresh dill, basil, thyme. Pulse and add 3/4 pound cream cheese. Pulse and add just a little bit of milk for spreading.

Lemon Thyme Potato Pancakes

These unusual potato pancakes are delicious even in the morning with applesauce. The inn serves them this way and tops them with crème fraîche. They are also good with sour cream or plain yogurt and sweet applesauce.

2	large Russet potatoes, peeled		$1/2$	teaspoon salt
$1/2$	yellow onion, peeled		$1/2$	teaspoon fresh minced lemon thyme
2	eggs, slightly beaten			
2	tablespoons all-purpose flour		$1/4$ to $1/3$	cup unsalted butter
$1/2$	teaspoon freshly grated nutmeg			Fresh lemon thyme sprigs for garnish
$1/4$	teaspoon freshly cracked white pepper			

MAKES 6 SERVINGS

Using a hand grater, shred the potatoes and the onion onto a clean kitchen towel. Twist and squeeze the towel to remove as much moisture as possible. Place the shredded mixture in a large bowl and add the eggs, flour, nutmeg, pepper, salt, and lemon thyme.

Preheat the oven to 150°. In a heavy skillet, melt a spoonful of butter until it foams. Drop small mounds of the potato mixture into the skillet. With a spatula, shape the potato mixture into flat circles, about 3 inches in diameter and $1/2$-inch thick. Fry until the undersides are golden brown. Flip the pancakes and continue to cook, occasionally pressing down with the spatula, about 4 to 6 minutes. Repeat with the remaining potato mixture, adding more butter for each batch. Keep warm in preheated oven. Garnish with sprigs of lemon thyme.

—THE JOHNSON HOUSE

Herb-Scented Stuffed Onion Saucers

Onions stuffed with mushrooms, capers, rosemary, and parsley offer a stunning appetizer or side dish.

Other great enhancements for tomato sandwiches: Feta cheese, mayonnaise, mustard, celery seeds, toasted papaya seeds, cream cheese and black olives, fresh Mozzarella cheese, roasted garlic.

3	large Spanish onions, peeled	1	tablespoon fresh rosemary, finely minced
3	slices day-old Italian bread		
1/2	cup skim milk	2	cloves garlic, minced
2	egg whites, lightly beaten	1/2	teaspoon salt
3 to 4	large portobello mushrooms (about 1/2 pound), finely chopped	1/2	teaspoon freshly cracked black pepper
		1/4	cup fine dry bread crumbs
2	tablespoons capers, drained and minced	1 1/2	teaspoons olive oil
1	tablespoon fresh parsley, chopped		

MAKES 6 SERVINGS

Carefully trim the root and flower ends of the onions, so that they sit flat. Cook the onions in simmering water for 10 minutes.

Soak the bread slices in milk for 10 minutes. Press the bread through a strainer to remove excess liquid. Break into small pieces.

Preheat the oven to 350°. In a large mixing bowl, combine the moistened bread, egg whites, mushrooms, capers, parsley, rosemary, garlic, salt, and pepper. Mix well.

Slice the onions in half through the center. Scoop out the small center rings, leaving 2 or 3 outer rings intact. Coarsely chop the onion centers and add to the bread mixture.

Fill the reserved onion shells with the stuffing and arrange them in a shallow baking dish. Sprinkle with dry bread crumbs and oil. Bake for 25 minutes, or until the tops are golden brown.

—THE CAPTAIN FREEMAN INN

Rosemary Biscotti

❧

Dunk this savory biscotti into garden soups or serve with a tomato chutney. It is also great alone as an hors d'oeuvre or as the bread you are serving with a complementary meal. This recipe has a nice crunchy texture and intense flavor.

2½	cups all-purpose flour, plus extra for rolling	⅔	cup sugar	
1½	teaspoons baking powder	2	eggs, whipped until pale yellow	
⅛	teaspoon salt	2	tablespoons anisette liqueur	
4	sprigs fresh rosemary, stemmed and minced		Rosemary sprigs for garnish	
⅓	cup (¾ stick) unsalted butter at room temperature			

MAKES 24 BISCOTTI

Preheat the oven to 350°. Over a small bowl sift the flour, baking powder, and salt; mix in the rosemary and set aside. In the bowl of an electric mixer fitted with a paddle (or regular beaters), combine the butter and sugar and beat on medium-high speed until light and creamy. Gradually add the eggs, incorporating after each addition. Add the anisette slowly; mix until combined. Reduce speed to low and gradually add the flour mixture. Continue mixing on medium speed until the dough is stiff but slightly sticky.

Place the dough on a lightly floured surface and cut in half. Roll each into a cylinder, about 2½ inches in diameter. Place the logs 3 inches apart on a greased and floured parchment-lined baking pan. Place in the oven for 30 minutes or until a light golden brown. Leave the oven on but let the biscotti cool and then cut diagonally into ½-inch slices. Lay the sliced biscotti cut-side down in a single layer and return to the oven to bake for 10 minutes more. Remove and set aside to cool. Serve garnished with rosemary sprigs.

—GAIL'S KITCHEN

LEFT: FACING THE MOON WHILE ONE SLEEPS IN THE MOONFLOWER ROOM AT THE WILDFLOWER INN

Posies
for the
Palate

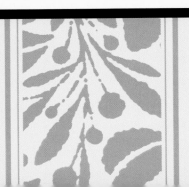

Lemon Flower Pancakes with Pansy Butter

The inn's slogan states, ". . . where the little things count." Innkeepers Donna and Phil Stone live up to it and more. When asked about my favorite inns, this is always at the top. Pancakes with flowers are poetry on the breakfast table. Donna truly enjoys cooking and decorating, too, as the inn's Jasmine Room (left) shows.

PICTURE FACING CHAPTER OPENER: POTATO AND
HERB SOUP WITH CALENDULA; RECIPE ON PAGE 95

Butter

¹/₂	cup (1 stick) butter, softened
¹/₂	cup fresh pansies, plus more for garnish

Batter

8	eggs, separated
¹/₂	cup sugar
1	cup lemon yogurt
1	cup milk
2	teaspoons lemon extract

2	teaspoons grated lemon peel
3	cups unbleached, all-purpose flour
2	teaspoons baking soda
1	teaspoon salt
1	teaspoon freshly ground nutmeg
¹/₂	cup fresh flower petals such as calendula, dianthus, or marigolds
	Fresh berry sauce

MAKES 6 SERVINGS

*P*repare the butter. Cream together the butter and flowers. Roll into a log and refrigerate. When ready to serve, garnish with pansies.

Prepare the pancakes. In a large bowl of electric mixer, beat together egg yolks and sugar for about 3 to 4 minutes until thick and pale yellow. Whisk the yogurt, milk, lemon extract, and lemon peel into the egg mixture.

In another, bowl sift together the flour, baking soda, salt, and nutmeg. Set aside.

Using clean beaters, whip the egg whites in another bowl until stiff peaks form. Whisk the flour mixture into the egg-and-yogurt mixture, just until smooth. Fold in the egg whites. Then fold in the flower petals.

Pour the batter (to form 3-inch pancakes) on a preheated griddle and cook until the tops bubble. Flip and cook on the other side for about 1 minute more. Pancakes should be golden. Do not overcook.

Serve with a fresh berry sauce of choice or maybe syrup and the pansy butter.

—THE WILDFLOWER INN

Potato and Herb Soup with Calendula

〜o〜

The petals of calendula flowers may not grow as prolifically as those of another choice for this soup—marigolds. Sprinkle either calendula or marigolds over this soup.

1	tablespoon butter
1	small onion, finely diced
1½	pounds white potatoes, peeled and cut into large cubes
1¾	cups chicken or vegetable stock
1¾	cups milk
	Salt and freshly cracked black pepper

⅛	teaspoon nutmeg
¼	cup finely chopped herbs in season
2	tablespoons calendula petals plus more for garnish
	Plain yogurt or whipped cream for garnish

MAKES 4 SERVINGS

Melt the butter in a large soup pot over medium-high heat. Add the onions. Cover and cook until the onions are translucent. Add the potatoes and cook for 2 to 3 minutes more. Add the stock and the milk. Simmer over low heat until the potatoes are very soft, about 15 minutes. Season with salt, pepper, and nutmeg. Transfer the soup to a food processor and purée until smooth. Stir in the fresh herbs and calendula petals. Garnish individual bowls with a dollop of plain yogurt or whipped cream, if desired, and calendula petals.

—THE NOTCHLAND INN

SPOTLIGHT ON CALENDULA

Chilled Spiced Peach Soup with Floating Violets

❧

Crystallizing flowers allows them to last longer and hold their shape. In this recipe, they make a splash finish to a delicious soup. Begin preparing the flowers a day or two ahead of serving time.

Candied Crystallized Violets	
1	egg white
1/2	teaspoon water
1	cup fresh violet blossoms
	Granulated sugar for dipping

Soup	
1 1/4	cups water
1/3	cup brandy

1/3	cup sugar
6	large peaches, washed, peeled, pitted, and sliced
1	teaspoon cinnamon
1/2	teaspoon grated fresh ginger
1/4	teaspoon nutmeg
3/4	cup freshly squeezed orange juice

MAKES 4 TO 6 SERVINGS

To make the candied crystallized violets, combine the egg white and the water in a mixing bowl. Beat until the white is fluffy—but not stiff. Dip the violets, top-side down, into the egg mixture, coating the entire blossom. Carefully dredge the flower in the sugar, covering completely. Arrange the candied blossoms on waxed paper and allow them to dry for 24 to 48 hours. Store the flowers between sheets of waxed paper in a tightly sealed container.

Prepare the soup. In a large saucepan, combine the water, brandy, and sugar over medium heat, stirring frequently. When the mixture is thick and syrupy, add the peaches, cinnamon, ginger, and nutmeg. Cover and simmer for 20 minutes. Remove from the heat and add the orange juice. Transfer the mixture to a blender, and purée until smooth. Chill for an hour or so. Serve cold in chilled clear cups. Garnish with candied crystallized violets.

—THE INN AT MAPLEWOOD FARM

Orange and Poppy-Seed Biscotti

≈

Shaped like crescent moons, biscotti evoke simple pleasures. And when Carol Covitz — chef and innkeeper at The Captain Freeman — showed me this recipe, I had to have it.

2	cups all-purpose flour
1	cup sugar
1/4	cup poppy seeds
1	teaspoon baking powder
1/2	teaspoon baking soda
1/4	teaspoon salt
2	eggs

2	egg whites
3	tablespoons freshly grated orange peel
1	tablespoon orange juice concentrate

MAKES 2 1/2 DOZEN

Preheat the oven to 325°. In a large mixing bowl, combine the flour, sugar, poppy seeds, baking powder, soda, and salt. In a separate bowl, whisk together the eggs, egg whites, orange peel, and orange juice concentrate. Add the wet ingredients to the dry ingredients and mix well.

Transfer the dough to a baking sheet and shape into 2 rectangles, each about 14 inches long, 3 inches wide, and 1/2 inch thick. Be sure rectangles are 4 inches apart.

Bake for 20 to 25 minutes, or until slightly brown and firm in the center. Cool on a wire rack for 10 minutes. Turn the oven down to 300°.

Cut the rectangles, on a slight diagonal, into 1/2-inch-thick slices. Arrange the slices—cut side up—on a baking sheet. Bake for 30 minutes. Cool on a wire rack and store in an airtight container.

—THE CAPTAIN FREEMAN INN

Buttermilk Lavender Bread

Maine is known for its prolific fields of lavender, which inspired this bread by the Belmont. You may substitute rosemary for the lavender. The recipe calls for spraying the loaves now and then with water to make a crustier bread. Be sure to use fresh lavender to intensify the flavor.

Prepare a dandelion salad for two: In a medium saucepan, boil 2 quarts water with 2 cups dandelions (leaves and crowns) for 5 minutes. Drain and toss with 1/4 cup olive oil, 1/4 cup balsamic or mint vinegar, 1 tablespoon honey, 1 minced garlic clove; and salt and pepper to taste.

3¹/₄	teaspoons active dry yeast	1	tablespoon, plus 1 teaspoon salt
1	cup lukewarm water		
1	cup buttermilk	6³/₄	cups all-purpose flour
¹/₃	cup olive oil		Yellow cornmeal
¹/₄	cup fresh lavender leaves, finely chopped		Coarse salt

MAKES 2 LOAVES

*S*tir the yeast into the lukewarm water and let stand until foamy, about 10 minutes. In the bowl of an electric mixer, combine the yeast mixture, buttermilk, olive oil, lavender, and salt. Mix until well blended. Gradually add the flour, beating on low speed until it is incorporated and a dough begins to form. Insert dough hook and knead on low speed for about 3 minutes. Transfer the dough to a floured surface and knead by hand until smooth and elastic, about 2 minutes. Place the dough in an oiled bowl, turning once to coat. Cover with plastic and allow the dough to rise in a warm place until double in size, about 1¹/₂ hours.

Turn the dough onto a floured surface and divide it into 2 sections. Shape each half into a round and place on a greased baking sheet coated with cornmeal. Cover the loaves with a damp towel and let rise for 1 hour.

Preheat the oven to 425°. With a serrated knife, gently carve a large asterisk into the surface of each loaf. Sprinkle with coarse salt. Bake for 15 minutes, occasionally spraying the loaves with water. Continue baking for 40 minutes, until golden brown, and hollow when tapped. Cool completely before serving.

—THE BELMONT INN

*N*ot all flowers are edible; some are poisonous. Eat only flowers that have been grown without pesticides. Eat primarily the petals of most flowers since the stamens and pistils are tougher.

Onion Yogurt Tart with Calendula Petals

੭੦ᴗᴄ

The topping of yogurt, caraway, and edible flowers offers your mealtime guests a special treat, and what a surprise—almost like a garden pizza.

Pastry

1/4	ounce dry yeast
1 1/2	cups lukewarm water
4 to 6	cups bread flour
1	teaspoon salt
1/4	cup cold unsalted butter (1/2 stick), cut into small pieces
3	eggs

Filling

3	tablespoons olive oil
4	cups thinly sliced onions
1/2	cup finely chopped dried tomatoes
1	teaspoon caraway seeds
4	eggs
1	cup plain yogurt

Assembly

2	tablespoons calendula petals

MAKES 8 TO 12 SERVINGS

*P*reheat the oven to 375°. Prepare the crust. Stir the yeast into the warm water and allow it to proof—about 10 minutes. In a food processor, blend together the flour, salt, and butter until coarse crumbs form. In a separate bowl, combine the yeast mixture and the eggs. Beat well, then add it to the flour mixture. Process until the ingredients are thoroughly mixed. Transfer the dough to a lightly floured surface, and knead until soft and pliable. Set it aside to rise in a

warm place until double in size. With a wooden rolling pin, roll the dough into a 14-inch circle, about 1/4-inch thick. Roll the outer edge with your hands like a pizza crust, giving the tart a 2-inch border all around. Set aside.

Prepare the filling. Heat the olive oil in a large skillet. Add the onions and cook until they just begin to brown. Add the dried tomatoes and cook for 2 minutes. Spread the onion mixture over the prepared pastry crust. Sprinkle with caraway seeds.

In a mixing bowl, beat together the eggs and the yogurt. Spread over the onion mixture. Sprinkle the calendula over the pie. Bake 30 to 40 minutes, or until the top is set and golden brown. Slice into pie wedges and serve warm or at room temperature.

—THE SETTLERS INN

Flower Petal Pound Cake

༄

Serve this with a glass of tea in the garden or on the porch and it feels like summer at any time of year. The colorful flower petals add some flavor and lots of interest to a basic pound cake that is more spongelike than most pound cakes.

A PEACEFUL SANCTUARY AFTER A DAY IN THE GARDEN: THE WILDFLOWER INN

1	cup (2 sticks) butter	1¹/₂	cups powdered sugar
1	teaspoon lemon extract	1	teaspoon baking powder
1¹/₂	cups all-purpose flour, sifted	1	cup assorted edible flower petals, torn into small pieces
5	eggs, separated		

MAKES 10 SERVINGS

Preheat the oven to 325°. In a large mixing bowl, cream the butter until light and fluffy. Stir in the lemon extract. Gradually beat in the flour.

In a separate bowl, beat the egg yolks until thick and lemon-colored. Slowly add the sugar, beating until smooth. Add the egg mixture to the flour mixture, stirring well.

In a clean bowl, whip the egg whites until stiff peaks form. Fold the whipped whites into the batter. Sift the baking powder over the mixture and beat thoroughly. Gently fold in the fresh flower petals.

Coat a 9x5-inch pan with cooking oil spray. Bake for 1 hour or until a tester comes clean.

— THE WILDFLOWER INN

Lavender Cookies

〜⚬〜

Lavender: Fragrance of Provence is a book that makes me feel like I'm holding a field of lavender in my hand, the way the author describes this delightful herb. But this is only imagery; so I take to the kitchen and create reality with these scrumptious, crowd-pleasing cookies first given to me by a friend.

1/2	cup vegetable shortening		1	teaspoon baking powder
1/2	cup (1 stick) butter		1	teaspoon vanilla extract
3	teaspoons freshly snipped lavender leaves, minced		1/2	teaspoon almond extract
2 1/4	cups all-purpose flour		1	handful lavender blossoms, coarsely chopped
1 1/4	cups sugar			
2	eggs			

MAKES 3 DOZEN COOKIES

*P*reheat the oven to 375°. In a large bowl of electric mixer, combine the shortening, butter, and lavender leaves. Beat at medium-high speed for about 30 seconds, until the mixture has softened. Add half of the flour. Add the sugar, eggs, baking powder, and vanilla and almond extracts. Beat until combined. Stir in the remaining flour. Gently fold in the lavender blossoms.

Drop by the rounded teaspoonful 2 inches apart onto ungreased, nonstick baking sheets. Bake for 8 to 10 minutes, or until the edges are golden. Cool on wire racks.

— GAIL'S KITCHEN

Get yourself a copy of Along the Garden Path *by innkeepers Bill & Sylvia Varney. It is loaded with posy ideas, recipes, and just good reading. Call the Varneys at their Fredericksburg Herb Farm in Fredericksburg, Texas.*

Directory

The Belmont Inn
6 Belmont Avenue
Camden, ME 04843
(207) 236-8053

Rooms: 6

Set on a quiet street in a village that looks like a picture postcard, the Belmont offers gracious, fine dining with an innovative menu by Chef Gerald Clare. Rooms are simple but elegantly appointed and maintained.

The Belvedere Mansion
PO Box 785
Rhinebeck, NY 12572
(914) 889-8000

Rooms: 11

Romance seems to be around every corner—from the private cottage rooms to the wood-burning fireplaces in the dining room and even the petite tea room. The mansion overlooks a majestic spot along the Hudson River.

A Cambridge House
2218 Massachusetts Avenue
Cambridge, MA 02140
(617) 491-6300

Rooms: 16

While the city whirls excitedly around it, inside, A Cambridge House complements the Boston sophistication in its decor and service. Afternoon hors d'oeuvres are a meal in themselves. Breakfast is plentiful and delicious. Fresh tea, coffee, and fruit can always be found in the parlor. This is a prime example of America's best urban inns.

The Captain Freeman Inn
15 Breakwater Road
Brewster, Cape Cod, MA 02631
(508) 896-7481

Rooms: 12

In the late 1860s, Captain William Freeman built this mansion in the charming Cape Cod village of Brewster. At the time, the city was home to more deepwater captains than anywhere else in America. The historic and romantic inn offers a variety of accommodation options.

PICTURE FACING DIRECTORY OPENER: NOTCHLAND INN

Diamond District B&B
142 Ocean Street
Lynn, MA 01902
(617) 599-4470

Rooms: 8

Have a full breakfast on antique English china with a view of the ocean from this Georgian-style clapboard mansion. You'll forget the issue of the day and focus on what really matters.

Harbor House Inn by the Sea
5600 S. Highway 1
Box 369
Elk, CA 95432
(707) 877-3203

Rooms: 10

The inn is made from redwood with a deck of the same material, overlooking a fairytale cove and water, water everywhere. The water smashing upon the rocky shore is a natural alarm clock. Gardens are everywhere to enjoy—one spilling over with vegetables, another with neat and tidy herbs, and a tangled one of wild berries and calla lilies.

The Inn at Cedar Falls
21190 State Route 374
Logan, Ohio 43138
(614) 385-7489

Rooms: 12

Gardens surround diners sitting out in warm weather on the patio outside the inn's cozy, log-style dining room. Flowers skirt the edge of a hill that reaches up to the fenced garden, alive with a variety of vegetables, herbs, and flowers.

The Inn at Maplewood Farm
447 Center Road
Hillsborough, NH 03244
(603) 464-4242

Rooms: 5

Old radio shows hum quietly through the speakers of antique radios collected by innkeeper Jayme Simoes. The setting is as tranquil as listening to these shows on the radio next to your bed. This is the kind of gem of a true New England bed-and-breakfast that gets you hooked on staying only at small inns when you travel.

The Inn at Meadowbrook
Cherry Lane Road
East Stroudsburg, PA 18301
(717) 629-0296

Rooms: 16

    All sorts of equestrian trappings surround the inn. Take to the trails or write out postcards by the reflecting pond. Food is full of character and carefully considered. Popovers, the size and suppleness of an equestrian's glove, are served brown and bountiful each evening.

The Inn at Ormsby Hill
Historic Route. 7A
Manchester Center, VT 05255
(802) 362-1163

Rooms: 10

    A gracious manor house built around 1760, this inn spells comfort and historic charm. Innkeepers Chris and Ted Sprague formerly owned the Newcastle Inn in Maine where Chris was well known for her fine cuisine. Her reputation and fine food are now ensconced at Ormsby Hill.

The Johnson House
216 Maple Street
Box 1892
Florence, OR 97439

Rooms: 3

    A century-old home is host to feather beds with eyelet comforters and antiques. A rose-and-lavender border scallops a walk to one of the guest cottages. Old-fashioned geraniums serve up color in an ambitious herb garden full of pineapple sage and pennyroyal.

The Littlepage Inn
15701 Monrovia Road
Mineral, VA 23117
(703) 854-9861

Rooms: 4

    This 1811 plantation home, with heart-pine floors and grain-painted doors, is full of character and refinement. Views are spectacular and the breakfast is well known for its creative dishes.

Mast Farm Inn
Box 704
Valle Crucis, NC 28691
(704) 963-5857

Rooms: 12

Everything blooms for the table here at this historic inn that dates as early as the 1700s. Salad ingredients are grown in rows across from the main house and there are other vegetables growing everywhere. You can hear the corn whisper in this quiet valley.

The Notchland Inn
Hart's Location, NH 03812
(603) 374-6131

Rooms: 11

Literally tucked into the Mount Washington range and its environs, this comfortable Gustav Stickley-style inn is a peaceful getaway. How about a gazebo by the pond or a wood-fired hot tub from which to watch the stars? The 1860s granite mansion hosts outbuildings and garden courtyards.

The Nuthatch B&B
7161 Edgewater Place
Indianapolis, IN 46240
(317) 257-2660

Rooms: 2

Innkeeper Joan Hamilton Morris is a cooking school instructor with great ideas for recipes. Herbal and vegetarian breakfasts are the order of the day here and you can have a tour of the herb garden. The Wren's Nest guest room is a hideaway room with clawfoot tub and a small deck off an herbal garden that fills the senses.

October Country Inn
PO Box 66
Bridgewater Corners, VT 05035
(802) 672-3412

Rooms: 10

Dishes that are curious, reverent, and full of sincere flavor are the hallmarks of the family-style dining at this inn. Traditions are as strong as the emphasis on simplicity and comfort. Anytime of year, this is an inn that offers the best of what life is really all about.

Pederson Victorian B&B
1782 Highway 120 North
Lake Geneva, WI 53147
(414) 248-9110

Rooms: 4

Vegetarian breakfasts are a mainstay at this 1880 hideaway. It is all here—white gingerbread trim, front-porch swing, storage for your bicycle, and plenty of backyard hammocks.

The Red Hook Inn
31 South Broadway
Red Hook, NY 12571
(914) 758-8445

Rooms: 5

The Hudson Valley is enchanting, and at its center is this charming Federal-style inn dating to 1842. Breakfast and dinner are served here just as they have been for more than fifty years. Before that time, this was a private residence.

The Settlers Inn
Four Main Avenue
Hawley, PA 18428
(717) 226-2993

Rooms: 18

Regional cooking—with local, organic produce and herbs from the innkeeper's garden—is the signature of this traditional mountain-style country inn. Breads are sold daily from the check-in desk for locals and tourists alike.

The Wildflower Inn
167 Palmer Avenue
Falmouth, MA 02540
(508) 548-9524

Rooms: 6

Donna and Phil Stone brought this 1910 seaside home back to life, and what a life they gave it: from theme guest rooms, decorated with such good taste—warm, friendly, and very unusual—to breakfasts so pleasing to the eye that guests want to photograph dishes before eating. The inn is a great home base for day trips to Martha's Vineyard. Do not miss a moonlit walk to town or a bike ride along the coastal trail.

Index